Torringford School LMC
800 Charles Street
Torrington, CT 06790
(860)489-2300

Explore and Draw

MOTORCYCLES

DRAWING AND READING

Gare Thompson

ROURKE
PUBLISHING

www.rourkepublishing.com

Editor: Penny Dowdy
Art Direction: Cheena Yadav (Q2AMedia)
Designer: Suzena Samuel (Q2AMedia)
Illustrator: Samar Jyoti Das
Picture researcher: Hartej Kour (Q2AMedia)

Picture credits:
t=top b=bottom c=centre l=left r=right
Cover: CTR Photos/Shutterstock.
Back Cover: Rod Kaye/Istockphoto, Roessler Carl/Photolibrary, Tischenko Irina/Shutterstock, Cretolamna/Shutterstock, Nathan Jones/Istockphoto, David Lewis/Istockphoto, Malou Leontsinis/Shutterstock, Radoslav Stoilov/Shutterstock, Close Encounters Photography/Shutterstock, CTR Photos/Shutterstock, Apdesign/Shutterstock.
Title Page: Luis Louro/Shutterstock, Marcel Jancovic/Shutterstock, Inc/Shutterstock, Vitaly Romanovich/Shutterstock, Dmitry Nikolaev/Shutterstock, Ariadna De Raadt/Shutterstock, David Huntley/Shutterstock, Adisa/Shutterstock, Ramzi Hachicho/Shutterstock, Sergey Ryzhov/Shutterstock, Ljupco Smokovski/Shutterstock, Subbotina Anna/Shutterstock.
Insides: Luis Louro/Shutterstock, Marcel Jancovic/Shutterstock, Inc/Shutterstock, Vitaly Romanovich/Shutterstock, Dmitry Nikolaev/Shutterstock, Ariadna De Raadt/Shutterstock, David Huntley/Shutterstock, Adisa/Shutterstock, Ramzi Hachicho/Shutterstock, Sergey Ryzhov/Shutterstock, Ljupco Smokovski/Shutterstock, Subbotina Anna/Shutterstock. Luis Louro/Shutterstock, Marcel Jancovic/Shutterstock, Inc/Shutterstock, Vitaly Romanovich/Shutterstock, Dmitry Nikolaev/Shutterstock, Ariadna De Raadt/Shutterstock, David Huntley/Shutterstock, Adisa/Shutterstock, Ramzi Hachicho/Shutterstock, Sergey Ryzhov/Shutterstock, Ljupco Smokovski/Shutterstock, Subbotina Anna/Shutterstock: 4- 24, Mercedes-Benz Classic: 6, Mary Evans Picture Library/Photolibrary: 7, Sergey Kamshylin/Shutterstock: 10, Knud Nielsen/Shutterstock: 11, Steven Robertson/Istockphoto: 14, David Kohl/AP Photo: 15, Todd Tankersley/PiCycle 2009: 18, Image courtesy of Intelligent Energy plc : 19.

Q2AMedia Art Bank: Cover, Back Cover, Title Page, 4-5, 8-9, 12-13, 16-17, 20-21.

Library of Congress Cataloging-in-Publication Data

Becker, Ann, 1965 Oct. 6-
Motorcycles: explore and draw / Gare Thompson.
p. cm. – (Explore and draw)
Includes index.
ISBN 978-1-61590-257-6 (hard cover)
ISBN 978-1-61590-497-6 (soft cover)
1. Motorcycles in art–Juvenile literature. 2. Drawing–Technique–Juvenile literature.
I. Title. II. Title: Explore and draw.
NC825.A4B43 2009
743'.8962913334–dc22
2009021617

Rourke Publishing
Printed in the United States of America, North Mankato, Minnesota
033010
033010LP

www.rourkepublishing.com - rourke@rourkepublishing.com
Post Office Box 643328 Vero Beach, Florida 32964

Contents

Technique

Ovals, triangles, crescents, circles, and tubes are the basic shapes used to draw motorcycles. Think about which ones to use to draw your motorcycle.

1

Start by drawing a long backline. Use it as your guide. Then draw two large circles below it. These are the wheels. Add a large triangle between the wheels for the engine space.

2

Draw bigger circles around the small circles for the wheels. Add ovals for the gas tank and the seat and a circle for the light. Draw tubes for the frame of the motorcycle.

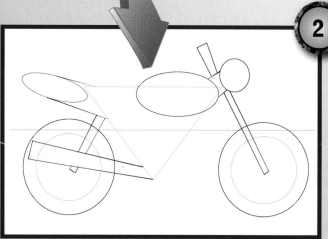

3

Draw in the major parts of the motorcycle, including the engine, gas tank, exhaust pipe, fenders, handlebars, and seat. Connect all the parts to form the complete **framework** of the motorcycle.

4

Smooth out the lines. Erase any extra lines. Give the seat a softer shape. Add small details to the motorcycle, such as spokes on the wheels, a gas cap, lights, or brake wires, for a more finished drawing.

5

Shade the various motorcycle parts with light and dark tones to give them dimension.

Early History of Motorcycles

Early motorcycles were like bicycles with motors. Many different people worked to create the motorcycles we see today. Here are some of the early **inventors**.

Early Inventors

Two men built the first motorcycles. They were Sylvester Howard Roper and Gottlieb Daimler. Roper lived in the United States. In 1867, he attached a steam engine to his bike. He toured circuses and fairs with his machine. Roper never **patented** his work.

So, many people built steam engines for bikes. Today, you can see Roper's bike in the Smithsonian Museum.

Daimler was an engineer. He lived in Germany. In 1885, he and a friend built a gas engine. They attached it to a bike. They called the motorbike a riding carriage.

Early motorcycles were bikes with motors.

First Motorcycles For Sale

In the late 1880s, many bike makers **adapted** their bikes to work with new and powerful engines. People loved the motorized bikes. Some bikes went over 50 miles per hour (80.46 kilometers per hour). These new bikes were called "motor cycles."

Early motorcycles looked like moving steam engines.

VELOCIPEDO DE VAPOR.

Draw an Early Motorcycle

The first motorcycles were more like bicycles with motors.

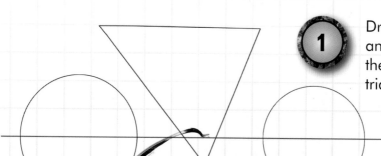

1. Draw a ground line and two circles for the tires. Then draw a triangle between them.

2. Draw a circle at the bottom of the triangle for the pedals. Draw smaller circles inside the tires for wheels. Next, draw tubes from the center of the wheels to the top of the triangle to form the frame.

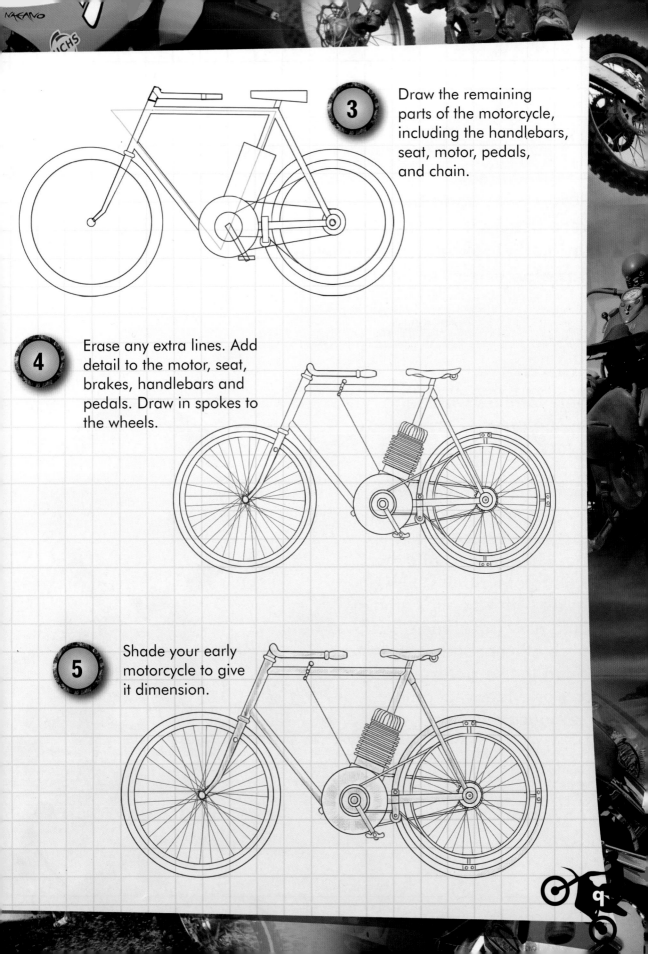

3 Draw the remaining parts of the motorcycle, including the handlebars, seat, motor, pedals, and chain.

4 Erase any extra lines. Add detail to the motor, seat, brakes, handlebars and pedals. Draw in spokes to the wheels.

5 Shade your early motorcycle to give it dimension.

Types of Motorcycles

Motorcycles soon became popular. They were used for travel, work, and, of course, fun! Let's look at three different kinds of motorcycles.

Sidecars

Some families wanted to buy motorcycles instead of cars. Motorcycles were cheaper, but they were also smaller. How could a family fit? The answer was to build **sidecars**. A sidecar is a one-wheeled cart attached to a motorcycle. It is like a basket with wheels. Families could now travel together. Police officers and soldiers began to use sidecars for work. Today, people use sidecars for fun.

Armies used sidecars during World War II.

Scooters

Scooters became popular after World War II. Cars were expensive. People needed an easy, inexpensive way to get around. An inventor in Italy built a scooter in 1946. It became very popular. Today, many people use scooters. They are cheap to buy, easy to drive, and use less gas.

Touring Motorcycles

Touring motorcycles are great for people who want to ride the open road. These machines have wide windshields, big engines, and large fuel tanks. They are made for long trips. People use touring motorcycles to go camping and attend **rallies**. Rallies are held around the world in all kinds of weather and over every kind of **terrain**.

In Italy, scooters are called vespas. Vespa in Italian means wasp.

Draw a Sidecar

Sidecars have one wheel and are connected to the side of a motorcycle.

1 Draw a large oval for the sidecar. Add two smaller ovals for the wheels.

2 Add a large triangle as a guideline. Draw more ovals and a tube for the sidecar and motorcycle.

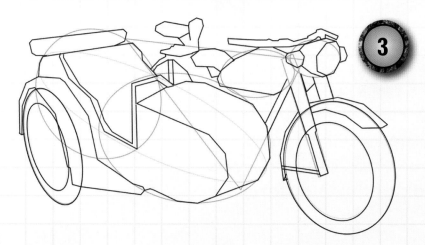

3 Draw the basic framework of the sidecar and the part of the motorcycle that shows.

4 Smooth the lines. Add details to the sidecar and motorcycle, including spokes to the wheels. Erase any extra lines.

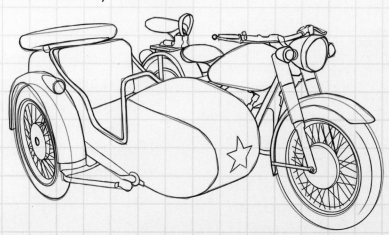

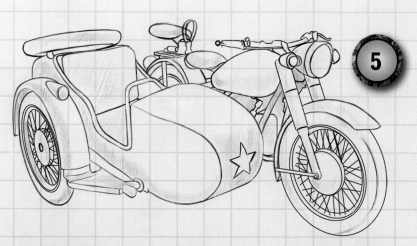

5 Shade your sidecar and motorcycle to make it look more realistic.

The Racers

People built motorcycles to race. There are many kinds of motorcycle races. Let's look at three different kinds of races.

Road Racing

The type of road race is determined by three things. First is the type of motorcycle ridden in the race. Next is the type of road. Third is the time and length of the race. One kind of race is the Motorcycle Grand Prix. Special motorcycles are made for this race.

Another kind of road race is the **endurance** race. This race tests the endurance, or strength, of the motorcycle and the driver. Some endurance races last as long as 24 hours. They use teams of two to four drivers.

In endurance races, drivers see how long they and their motorcycle can last.

Evel Knievel was a famous motorcycle jumper and daredevil.

Motocross Racing

Motocross racing is like road racing except it is done **off-road**. In these races, drivers speed across all kinds of terrain. They might drive on sand, mud, or grass. Many of the tracks have jumps. Drivers perform **daredevil** stunts through the air during the races.

Track Racing

In track racing teams or individuals race each other. The **opponents** ride around an oval track for a set number of **laps**. Track races are run on different surfaces. Some tracks use ice. Others use grass or wood. Racers drive special motorcycles that have no brakes!

Draw a Racing Motorcycle

Racing motorcycles look sleek and fast.

1 Draw a large triangle to form the base for the racing motorcycle. Add two large ovals for the wheels.

2 Draw ovals to form the windshield and framework of the motorcycle. Add a tube to connect the front wheel.

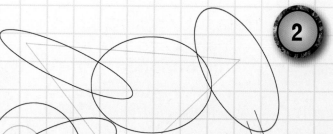

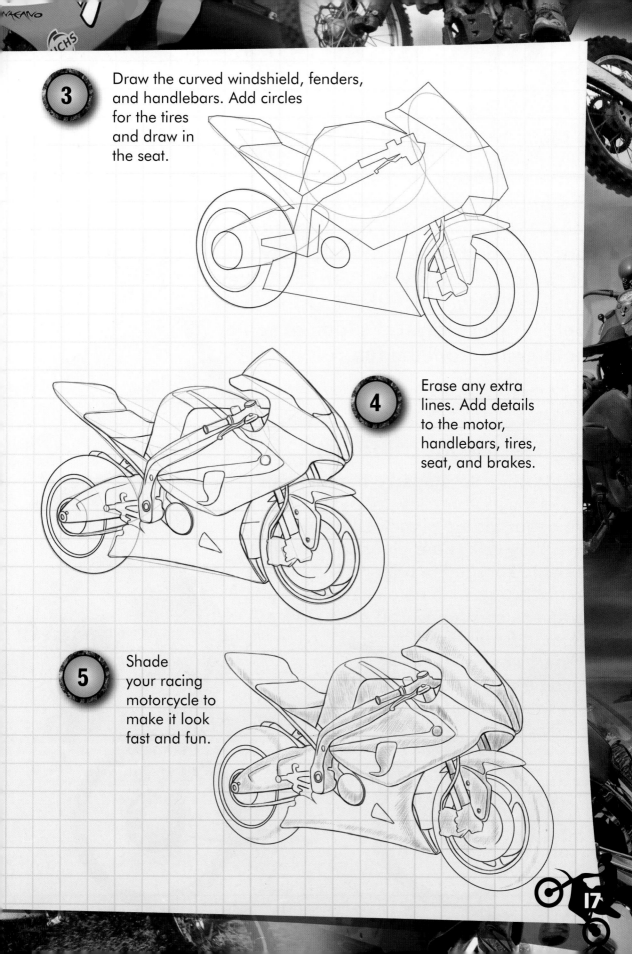

3 Draw the curved windshield, fenders, and handlebars. Add circles for the tires and draw in the seat.

4 Erase any extra lines. Add details to the motor, handlebars, tires, seat, and brakes.

5 Shade your racing motorcycle to make it look fast and fun.

The Future of Motorcycles

The future of motorcycles looks green. People are working to develop motorcycles that are good for the planet. They will be run on electricity or even air. Other motorcycles will be **hybrid**, using both fuel and electricity. Let's look at some motorcycles from the future.

The Electric Machine

People have developed different kinds of electric motorcycles. Many think they are better for the planet. Like electric cars, these bikes are plugged into an outlet to charge the battery. The bikes do not use gas. Some electric bikes go as fast as cars, up to 150 mph (241.40 kilometers per hour). These bikes have become a greener way to get around in cities.

People can buy an electric motorbike kit and build their own bike.

18

The air motorcycle looks like a moped.

Hybrid Motorcycles

Hybrid motorcycles are like hybrid cars. They save gas by using both fuel and electricity. They lower **pollution**. Many of these bikes use a high-powered battery that is charged when not in use. People think hybrid motorcycles will become as popular as hybrid cars.

Air Today

People are also trying to build motorcycles that run on air. Now that would be green and cheap! One man used a regular motorcycle to herd sheep. He kept **tinkering** with his machine. Finally, he invented the air motorcycle. His bike goes only 18 mph (28.96 kilometers per hour), but it does not pollute the air. Air motorcycles are not yet for sale, but they will be one day.

So what do you think the motorcycle of the future will be like?

Draw a New Motorcycle

You can create your own motorcycle design of the future by using these drawing steps.

1 Draw a midline. Add two large circles at each end and a large triangle above the line.

2 Add a smaller triangle to the top of the large triangle and a small circle to the bottom. Draw tubes to connect these shapes to the wheels.

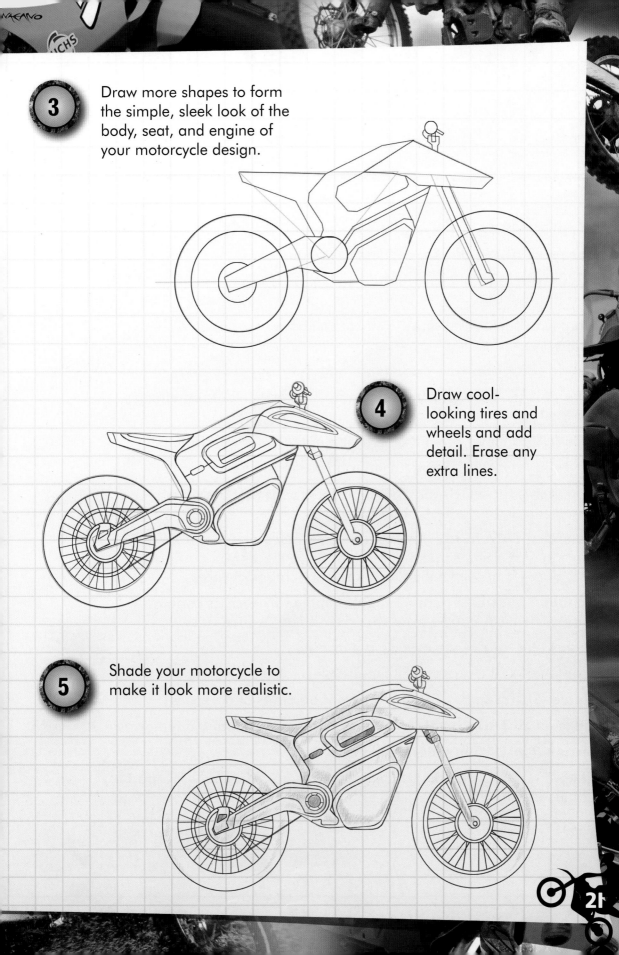

3 Draw more shapes to form the simple, sleek look of the body, seat, and engine of your motorcycle design.

4 Draw cool-looking tires and wheels and add detail. Erase any extra lines.

5 Shade your motorcycle to make it look more realistic.

Glossary

adapted (uh-DAPT-id): changed in order to make suitable

daredevil (DAYR-dev-il): reckless or dangerous

endurance (en-DUR-uns): the power to put up with hardships or difficulties

framework (FRAYM-wurk): a structure that gives shape or support to something

hybrid (HIGH-brid): a vehicle that operates using two kinds of fuel

inventors (in-VEN-turz): people who make or think of something for the first time

laps (LAPZ): times around or over the entire length of something

off-road (awf-ROHD): off paved roads or in rugged areas

opponents (un-POH-nuntz): people or groups that are against others in a fight, contest, or discussion

patented (PAT-unt-id): having received a piece of paper from the government giving someone the right to be the only one to make, use, or sell a new invention for a certain number of years

pollution (puh-LYEW-shun): harmful materials such as certain gases, chemicals, and wastes that dirty the air, water, or soil

rallies (RAL-eez): meetings for a purpose

scooters (SKOOT-urz): small motorcycles

shade (SHAYD): to mark with different amounts of darkness

sidecars (SIGHD-kahrz): one-wheeled carts attached to a motorcycle

terrain (tuh-RAYN): ground or land

tinkering (TING-kur-ing): making unskilled or experimental efforts at mechanical repair

Index

Websites to Visit

http://www.clubcycle.com
Gives information about motorcycles, including who invented them and how to ride them.

http://www.totalmotorcycle.com/future.htm
Tells the history of motorcycles and how manufacturers are planning for the future with hybrids and electric motorcycles.

http://auto.howstuffworks.com/motorcycle7.htm
Discover all you want to know about motorcycles and how they work.

About the Author
Gare Thompson has written over 200 children's books. He has also taught elementary school. He lives in Massachusetts with his wife. During the summer, he has gone on motorcycle rides with friends, although he doesn't have his own motorcycle.

About the Illustrator
Samar Jyoti Das has illustrated a number of children's books. He has a Bachelor in Applied Arts. Samar draws primarily realistic art. He loves drawing the world around him. He has been working for Q2A Media for one year.